TABLE OF CO

1. PAN-ROASTED CHICKEN WITH VEGETABLES AND DIJON JUS

2. CREAMY GARLIC CHICKEN SPANAKOPITA SKILLET

3. SWEET AND SAVORY CORN CASSEROLE

4. BUTTER-BASTED, PAN-SEARED THICK-CUT STEAKS

5. PERFECT PAN-SEARED PORK CHOPS

6. CRISPY BAKED PASTA WITH MUSHROOMS, SAUSAGE, AND PARMESAN CREAM SAUCE

7. EGGY PUDS (BREAKFAST YORKSHIRE PUDDINGS WITH BACON AND FRIED EGGS)

8. EASY NO-KNEAD OLIVE-ROSEMARY FOCACCIA WITH PISTACHIOS

9. FOOLPROOF PAN PIZZA

10. EXTRA-CRISPY BAR-STYLE TORTILLA PIZZA

11. SOUTHERN-STYLE UNSWEETENED CORNBREAD RECIPE

12. MOIST AND TENDER BROWN BUTTER CORNBREAD RECIPE

13. QUICK AND EASY SKILLET TAMALE PIE WITH BROWN BUTTER CORNBREAD CRUST RECIPE

14. ONE-SKILLET SALMON WITH CURRIED LEEKS AND YOGURT-HERB SAUCE RECIPE

15. PAN-ROASTED QUAIL WITH PLUM PAN SAUCE RECIPE

16. PAN-SEARED FLANK STEAK WITH PEACHES AND DANDELION GREENS RECIPE

17. FRENCH ONION STRATA (SAVORY BREAD PUDDING) RECIPE

18. BAKED EGGS WITH CREAMY GREENS, MUSHROOMS, AND CHEESE RECIPE

19. BROILED TANDOORI-STYLE CHICKEN WITH ALMONDS AND COUSCOUS RECIPE

20. CRISPY PORK SHOULDER HASH WITH CHARRED ASPARAGUS AND SERRANO CHILI RECIPE

21. CREAMY PASTA WITH MUSHROOMS (PASTA AI FUNGHI) RECIPE

22. CRISPY CHEESE- AND KIMCHI-TOPPED SKILLET RICE RECIPE

23. PAN FRIED POTATOES

24. BREAKFAST VEGETABLE SCRAMBLE

25. EASY SHAKSHUKA WITH FETA

5. Add stock to pot with chicken backbone. Bring to a simmer over high heat, reduce to lowest setting, cover, and let gently bubble while the chicken roasts.

6. Add remaining tablespoon oil to skillet and heat over high heat until lightly smoking. Add vegetable mixture. Top with chicken pieces, skin side-up. Transfer to oven. Roast until chicken breast pieces register 150°F and chicken legs register at least 165°F on an instant read thermometer, removing pieces and transferring them to a clean plate as they finish roasting, 20 to 45 minutes total.

7. When all the chicken pieces have finished roasting, add shallots to skillet with the vegetables and toss to combine. Return to oven and continue roasting, flipping vegetables occasionally, until vegetables and shallots are browned all over, about 10 minutes. Remove skillet from oven, add parsley, toss to coat, then place chicken directly on top of vegetables.

8. Strain simmering chicken broth mixture into a small saucepan or bowl. Whisk in butter, dijon mustard, lemon juice, and fish sauce. Season jus to taste with salt and pepper. Serve chicken and vegetables immediately, serving jus at the table.

PAN-ROASTED CHICKEN WITH VEGETABLES AND DIJON JUS

YIELD: serves 4

TOTAL TIME: 1 hours 15 minutes

ACTIVE TIME: 45 minutes

INGREDIENTS

- 16 fingerling or yellow new potatoes, scrubbed
- 3 large carrots, 2 peeled and cut into 1-inch faux tourné chunks, 1 roughly chopped, divided
- Kosher salt
- 16 brussels sprouts, split in half
- Freshly ground black pepper
- 4 tablespoons extra-virgin olive oil, divided
- 1 whole chicken (about 4 pounds), cut into 8 serving pieces, backbone reserved
- 1 cup dry white wine
- 1 whole onion, split in half
- 1 stalk celery, roughly chopped
- 3 to 4 sprigs fresh sage
- 2 bay leaves
- 2 cups homemade or store-bought low-sodium chicken stock
- 1 medium shallot, thinly sliced
- 2 tablespoons minced fresh parsley leaves
- 2 tablespoons unsalted butter
- 1 tablespoon Dijon mustard
- 1 tablespoon juice from 1 lemon
- 2 teaspoons fish sauce

DIRECTIONS

1. Place potatoes and faux tourné carrots in a medium saucepan, cover with cold salted water, bring to a boil, and simmer until just tender, about 10 minutes. Add brussels sprouts, season with salt and pepper, toss with 2 tablespoons olive oil, and set aside.

2. Transfer chicken backbone to now-empty saucepan. Add roughly chopped carrot, onion, celery, sage, and bay leaves. Set aside. Season chicken pieces thoroughly with salt and pepper.

3. Heat 1 tablespoon oil in a large cast iron skillet and over high heat until lightly smoking. Add chicken pieces skin side-down and cook, moving chicken as little as possible, until chicken skin is rendered and deep golden brown, 8 to 12 minutes, reducing heat if smoking excessively. Flip pieces as they finish and lightly brown second side, about 3 minutes longer. Transfer browned chicken pieces to a plate and set aside.

4. When all chicken is browned, add white wine to skillet and scrape up any browned bits with a wooden spoon. Transfer white wine to saucepan with chicken backbone.

4. Add feta cheese, scallions, and dill and stir, allowing the feta to melt. Remove from heat. Return chicken and spinach to skillet, mixing well. If the sauce has thickened too much, add more chicken stock to reach the desired consistency, keeping in mind that the mixture will thicken even more when baking in the oven. Season with salt and pepper.

5. Melt the remaining 2 tablespoons butter in a small saucepan or in the microwave. Lay a sheet of phyllo on a work surface. Brush with melted butter, then scrunch up the sheet and set it on top of the spinach mixture in the skillet. Repeat with remaining phyllo until the skillet is completely covered.

6. Bake until phyllo is golden and crisp on top, about 20 minutes. Remove from oven, garnish with additional dill, and serve warm.

CREAMY GARLIC CHICKEN SPANAKOPITA SKILLET

YIELD: serves 6 **TOTAL TIME:** 1 hours 00 minutes

ACTIVE TIME: 40 minutes

INGREDIENTS

1 pound fresh baby spinach leaves, washed

6 tablespoons unsalted butter, divided

1 1/2 pounds boneless, skinless chicken breasts or thighs, chopped into 1-inch chunks

Kosher salt and freshly ground black pepper

5 medium cloves garlic, minced

2 tablespoons all-purpose flour

1/2 cup homemade chicken stock or low-sodium broth, plus more as needed

1/2 cup half-and-half

6 ounces feta cheese, crumbled

3 scallions, white and light green parts only, chopped

1 small bunch dill, chopped, plus more for garnish

6 to 8 sheets phyllo dough, thawed and covered with a towel

DIRECTIONS

1. Heat a large cast iron skillet over medium heat. Add spinach, a handful at a time, until the pan is full; you may have to cook the spinach in batches to ensure that it cooks evenly. Turn the spinach often until just wilted, then transfer to a colander and press out as much water as you can. Continue until all of the spinach is wilted and pressed.

2. Pour off any excess water in the skillet and place back over medium heat. Melt 2 tablespoons butter in the pan and add chicken. Season with salt and pepper. Cook, turning once, until the edges are lightly golden, about 4 minutes. Remove from heat and set aside.

3. Preheat oven to 425°F. Melt 2 tablespoons butter in same skillet and add garlic. Cook until fragrant, about 1 minute, then mix in flour. Stir together until the mixture forms a golden paste. Whisk in 1/2 cup chicken stock. Cook, stirring often, until mixture is thickened and coats the back of a spoon. Whisk in half-and-half.

SWEET AND SAVORY CORN CASSEROLE

YIELD: serves 12   **TOTAL TIME:** 1 hours 00 minutes

ACTIVE TIME: 25 minutes

INGREDIENTS

- 2 tablespoons unsalted butter (1 ounce; 30g)
- 1 large onion, diced (about 1 1/4 cups; 7 ounces; 200g)
- 1 small bell pepper, diced (about 3/4 cup; 4 ounces; 110g)
- 2 tablespoons sugar (1 1/2 ounces; 40g)
- Scant 1/4 cup fresh sage (about 1/2 ounce; 15g), finely chopped
- 1 tablespoon Diamond Crystal kosher salt (1/4 ounce; 7g); for table salt, use half as much by volume or use the same weight
- 1 teaspoon sweet paprika
- 1/8 teaspoon cayenne
- 15 ounces fresh or frozen corn kernels (about 3 cups; 425g)
- 1/2 cup white or yellow cornmeal (2 1/2 ounces; 70g)
- 3 large eggs
- 1 1/4 cups milk, any percentage (10 ounces; 280g)
- 1/2 cup heavy cream (4 ounces; 115g)
- 1 cup finely shredded cheese (3 ounces; 85g), such as cheddar, Monterey Jack, or Parmesan

DIRECTIONS

1. Adjust oven rack to lower-middle position and preheat to 350°F (177°C). Melt butter in a 10-inch cast iron skillet over medium heat, then add onion, bell pepper, sugar, sage, salt, paprika, and cayenne. Cook, stirring, until onions are translucent and just beginning to brown, about 10 minutes, then add corn. Continue cooking, stirring frequently, until no water remains in skillet, another 8 to 10 minutes, then stir in cornmeal and remove from heat.

2. In a small bowl, whisk together eggs, milk, and cream, then pour into corn mixture. Stir well to combine, sprinkle with cheese, and bake until softly set, about 20 minutes. Turn on the broiler and broil only until lightly browned, just a minute or two more.

BUTTER-BASTED, PAN-SEARED THICK-CUT STEAKS

YIELD: serves 2 to 3   **TOTAL TIME:** 0 hours 25 minutes

ACTIVE TIME: 15 minutes

INGREDIENTS

1 large bone-in T-bone or ribeye steak (see note)

Kosher salt and freshly ground black pepper

1/4 cup (60ml) vegetable or canola oil

3 tablespoons (45g) unsalted butter

6 sprigs thyme or rosemary (optional)

1/2 cup finely sliced shallots (about 1 large; optional)

4. Continue flipping and basting until an instant-read thermometer inserted into thickest part of tenderloin side registers 120 to 125°F (49 to 52°C) for medium-rare or 130°F (54°C) for medium, 8 to 10 minutes total.

5. Immediately transfer steak to a large heatproof plate and pour pan juices on top. Let rest 5 to 10 minutes. Carve and serve.

DIRECTIONS

1. Carefully pat steak dry with paper towels. Season liberally on all sides, including edges, with salt and pepper. If desired, let steak rest at room temperature for 45 minutes, or refrigerated, loosely covered, up to 3 days (see note).

2. In a 12-inch heavy-bottomed cast iron skillet, heat oil over high heat until just beginning to smoke. Carefully add steak and cook, flipping frequently, until a pale golden-brown crust starts to develop, about 4 minutes total.

3. Add butter, herbs (if using), and shallot (if using) to skillet and continue to cook, flipping steak occasionally and basting any light spots with foaming butter. If butter begins to smoke excessively or steak begins to burn, reduce heat to medium. To baste, tilt pan slightly so that butter collects by handle. Use a spoon to pick up butter and pour it over steak, aiming at light spots.

PERFECT PAN-SEARED PORK CHOPS

YIELD: serves 2 **TOTAL TIME:** 1 day

ACTIVE TIME: 30 minutes

INGREDIENTS

- 2 bone-in pork rib chops, preferably blade-end, 1 1/2 inches thick (12 to 16 ounces each)
- 2 tablespoons kosher salt
- 1 1/2 teaspoons sugar
- Freshly ground black pepper
- 2 tablespoons vegetable oil
- 2 tablespoons butter
- 1 medium shallot, thinly sliced
- 8 sprigs fresh thyme

DIRECTIONS

1. Pat pork chops dry with a paper towel. Combine salt and sugar in a small bowl. Season pork chops generously on all sides with salt/sugar mixture. Transfer to a wire rack set in a rimmed baking sheet and refrigerate, uncovered, at least 8 hours and up to 24.

2. The next day, preheat oven to 250°F. Place baking sheet with pork chops in oven and cook until an instant read thermometer inserted into the center of the chops registers 100 to 110°F on for medium-rare, about 30 minutes, or 110 to 120°F for medium, about 35 minutes. To prevent overcooking, start checking temperature 5 to 10 minutes before suggested time. Remove from oven.

3. Heat oil in a large stainless steel or cast iron skillet over high heat heat until smoking. Place pork chops in skillet and cook, turning occasionally, until starting to brown, about 1 1/2 minutes. Add butter, shallots, and thyme to skillet. Continue cooking, spooning shallots and thyme on top of chops and basting with butter until golden brown on both sides and well-crusted, about 2 minutes longer. Stack pork chops with tongs, hold them on their sides, and sear the fat caps on the edges until crisp, about a minute. Remove pan from heat, transfer chops to a clean rack set in a rimmed baking sheet, and let rest for 3 to 5 minutes.

4. Just before serving, reheat dripping in pan until smoking. Pour hot drippings over chops. They should sizzle and crisp a bit. Serve immediately.

4. Add flour and cook, stirring, until a thin film begins to form on the bottom of the pan, about 1 minute. Slowly whisk in chicken broth followed by heavy cream. Bring to a simmer and cook until thickened, about 2 minutes. Stir in remaining grated cheese until melted. Stir in remaining parsley and chives. Stir in sausage. Season to taste with salt and lots of black pepper.

5. Adjust rack to 10 inches below broiler element and preheat broiler to high. Cook pasta in salted water according to package directions, removing it when still just shy of al dente. Drain, reserving 1 cup of cooking liquid. Return to pot. Add mushroom mixture and stir to combine, adding liquid to adjust consistency. Pasta should be very loose but not soupy. Return to cast iron skillet and top with bread crumbs. Broil until golden brown, rotating pan as necessary, 2 to 3 minutes. Serve immediately.

CRISPY BAKED PASTA WITH MUSHROOMS, SAUSAGE, AND PARMESAN CREAM SAUCE

YIELD: serves 4 to 6   **TOTAL TIME:** 0 hours 30 minutes
ACTIVE TIME: 30 minutes

INGREDIENTS

- 1 cup Panko-style bread crumbs
- 6 ounces grated Parmesan cheese
- 1/4 cup chopped fresh parsley leaves
- 2 tablespoons finely minced fresh chives
- 2 small shallots, finely minced (about 1/2 cup)
- 2 medium cloves garlic, minced (about 2 teaspoons)
- 2 tablespoons extra-virgin olive oil
- Kosher salt and freshly ground black pepper
- 2 tablespoons unsalted butter
- 8 ounces Italian sausage (mild or hot), removed from casings
- 1 pound mixed mushrooms (such as portobello, shiitake, and oyster), cleaned and thinly sliced
- 1 tablespoon soy sauce
- 1 tablespoon juice from 1 lemon
- 2 1/2 tablespoons all-purpose flour
- 2 cups homemade or store-bought low-sodium chicken stock
- 1 cup heavy cream
- 12 ounces fresh or 8 ounces dried ridged pasta such as rotini or campanelle

DIRECTIONS

1. Bring a large pot of salted water to a boil and keep at a bare simmer. Combine bread crumbs, 2 ounces cheese, half of parsley, half of chives, 1/4 of shallots, 1/4 of garlic, and olive oil in a medium bowl and massage with hands until combined. Season to taste with salt and pepper.

2. Melt butter in a large cast iron skillet over medium-high heat until foaming. Add sausage and cook, mashing it with a potato masher or a wooden spoon until broken up and well browned, about 7 minutes. Use a slotted spoon to transfer sausage to a small bowl, leaving fat behind.

3. Increase heat to high, add mushrooms to skillet, and cook, stirring frequently, until moisture has evaporated and mushrooms are well-browned, about 10 minutes. Add shallots and garlic and cook, stirring, until fragrant, about 30 seconds. Add soy sauce and lemon juice and stir to combine.

EGGY PUDS (BREAKFAST YORKSHIRE PUDDINGS WITH BACON AND FRIED EGGS)

YIELD: serves 2 to 4   **TOTAL TIME:** 0 hours 40 minutes

ACTIVE TIME: 15 minutes

INGREDIENTS

- 7 large eggs
- 110g flour (3 3/4 ounces; about 3/4 cup)
- 130g milk (4 1/2 ounces; about half cup plus 1 tablespoon)
- 22g water (3/4 ounce; 1 1/2 tablespoons)
- Kosher salt and freshly ground black pepper
- 8 ounces bacon, diced (see note)
- 2 ounces grated Parmesan or other hard cheese (optional)
- 1 tablespoon unsalted butter
- 2 tablespoons chopped fresh chives

DIRECTIONS

1. Combine 3 eggs, flour, milk, water, and 1/2 teaspoon salt in a medium bowl and whisk until a smooth batter is formed. Let batter rest at room temperature for at least 30 minutes. Alternatively, for best results, transfer to an airtight container and refrigerate batter overnight or for up to 3 days. Remove from refrigerator while you preheat the oven.

2. Adjust oven rack to center position and preheat oven to 450°F (230°C). Divide bacon evenly between two 7-inch or one 10-inch cast iron or oven-safe non-stick skillets. Cook over medium heat, stirring frequently, until bacon is crisp and browned, about 8 minutes. Pour batter into skillet(s) and immediately transfer to the oven. Bake until puffed and deep brown and crisped all over, 20 to 25 minutes, sprinkling edges and center with cheese for last 5 minutes if using.

3. Several minutes before puddings come out of the oven, fry remaining 4 eggs in butter over medium heat until desired texture is reached. Season to taste with salt and pepper. Serve Yorkshire puddings immediately with eggs placed inside, sprinkled with chives, and topped with Hollandaise (if using).

5. At the end of the 2 hours, dough should mostly fill the skillet up to the edge. Use your fingertips to press it around until it fills every corner, popping any large bubbles that appear. Lift up one edge of the dough to let any air bubbles underneath escape and repeat, moving around the dough until there are no air bubbles left underneath and the dough is evenly spread around the skillet. Spread olives and pistachios all over the surface of the dough and press down on them with your fingertips to embed slightly. Drizzle with remaining olive oil. Sprinkle with rosemary and coarse salt.

6. Transfer skillet to oven and bake until top is golden brown and bubbly and bottom is golden brown and crisp when you lift it with a thin spatula, 16 to 24 minutes. Using a thin spatula, loosen focaccia and peek underneath. If bottom is not as crisp as desired, place pan on a burner and cook over medium heat, moving the pan around to cook evenly until it is crisp, 1 to 3 minutes. Transfer to a cutting board, allow to cool slightly, slice, and serve. Extra bread should be stored in a brown paper bag at room temperature for up to 2 days. Reheat in a 300°F oven for about 10 minutes before serving.

EASY NO-KNEAD OLIVE-ROSEMARY FOCACCIA WITH PISTACHIOS

YIELD: serves 12 **TOTAL TIME:** 1 day

ACTIVE TIME: 15 minutes

INGREDIENTS

- 500 grams (17 1/2 ounces, about 3 1/4 cups) all-purpose or bread flour
- 15 grams (.5 ounces, about 1 tablespoon) kosher salt
- 4 grams (.15 ounces, about 1 teaspoon) instant yeast
- 325 grams (11 1/2 ounces, about 1 1/2 cups minus 1 tablespoon) water
- 1/4 cup extra-virgin olive oil, divided
- 4 ounces pitted green olives, sliced
- Coarse sea salt
- 1/4 cup roasted pistachios, roughly chopped or lightly pounded in a mortar and pestle
- 2 tablespoons fresh rosemary leaves, very roughly chopped

DIRECTIONS

1. Combine flour, salt, yeast, and water in a large bowl. Mix with hands or a wooden spoon until no dry flour remains. The bowl should be at least 4 to 6 times the volume of the dough to account for rising.

2. Cover bowl tightly with plastic wrap, making sure that edges are well-sealed, then let rest on the countertop for at least 8 hours and up to 24 hours. Dough should rise dramatically and fill bowl.

3. Sprinkle the top of the dough lightly with flour, then transfer it to a lightly-floured work surface. Form into a ball by holding it with well-floured hands and tucking the dough underneath itself, rotating it until it forms a tight ball.

6. Top each round of dough with 3/4 cup sauce, spreading sauce to the very edge with the back of a spoon. Sprinkle evenly with mozzarella cheese, all the way to the edges. Season with salt. Add other toppings as desired. Drizzle with olive oil and scatter a few basil leaves over the top of each pizza, if desired.

5. After 2 hours, dough should be mostly filling the pan up to the edges. Use your fingertips to press it around until it fills in every corner, popping any large bubbles that appear. Lift up one edge of the dough to let any air bubbles underneath escape, then repeat, moving around the dough until there are no air bubbles left underneath and the dough is evenly spread around the pan.

7. Transfer pan to oven and bake until top is golden brown and bubbly and bottom is golden brown and crisp when you lift it with a thin spatula, 12 to 15 minutes. Immediately sprinkle with grated Parmesan or Pecorino Romano cheese, if using. Using a thin spatula, loosen pizza and peek underneath. If bottom is not as crisp as desired, place pan over a burner and cook on medium heat, moving the pan around to cook evenly until it is crisp, 1 to 3 minutes. Remove the pizzas and transfer to a cutting board. Cut each pizza into 6 slices and serve immediately.

FOOLPROOF PAN PIZZA

YIELD: serves 10 **TOTAL TIME:** 10 to 26 hours

ACTIVE TIME: 15 minutes

INGREDIENTS

- 400g bread flour (14 ounces; about 2 1/2 cups), plus more for dusting
- 10g kosher salt (0.35 ounces; about 2 teaspoons), plus more for sprinkling
- 4g instant yeast (0.15 ounces; about 1 teaspoon), such as
- 275g water (9.5 ounces; about 1 cup plus 3 tablespoons)
- 8g extra-virgin olive oil (0.25 ounces; about 2 teaspoons), plus more to coat pans and for drizzling
- 1 1/2 cups pizza sauce, such as our New York–style pizza sauce
- 12 ounces grated full-fat, low moisture (dry) mozzarella cheese (see note)
- Toppings as desired
- Small handful torn fresh basil leaves (optional)
- 2 ounces grated Parmesan or Pecorino Romano cheese (optional)

DIRECTIONS

1. Combine flour, salt, yeast, water, and oil in a large bowl. Mix with hands or a wooden spoon until no dry flour remains.

2. Cover bowl tightly with plastic wrap, making sure that the edges are well sealed, then let rest at cool room temperature for at least 8 hours and up to 24. Dough should rise dramatically and fill bowl.

3. Sprinkle top of dough lightly with flour, then transfer it to a well-floured work surface. Divide dough into 2 pieces and form each into a ball by holding it with well-floured hands and tucking the dough underneath itself, rotating it until it forms a tight ball.

4. Pour 1 to 2 tablespoons oil in the bottom of two 10-inch cast iron skillets or round cake pans. Place 1 ball of dough in each pan and turn to coat evenly with oil. Using a flat palm, press dough around the pan, flattening it slightly and spreading oil around the entire bottom and edges of the pan. Cover tightly with plastic wrap and let dough sit at room temperature for 2 hours. After the first hour, adjust an oven rack to the middle position and preheat oven to 550°F (290°C).

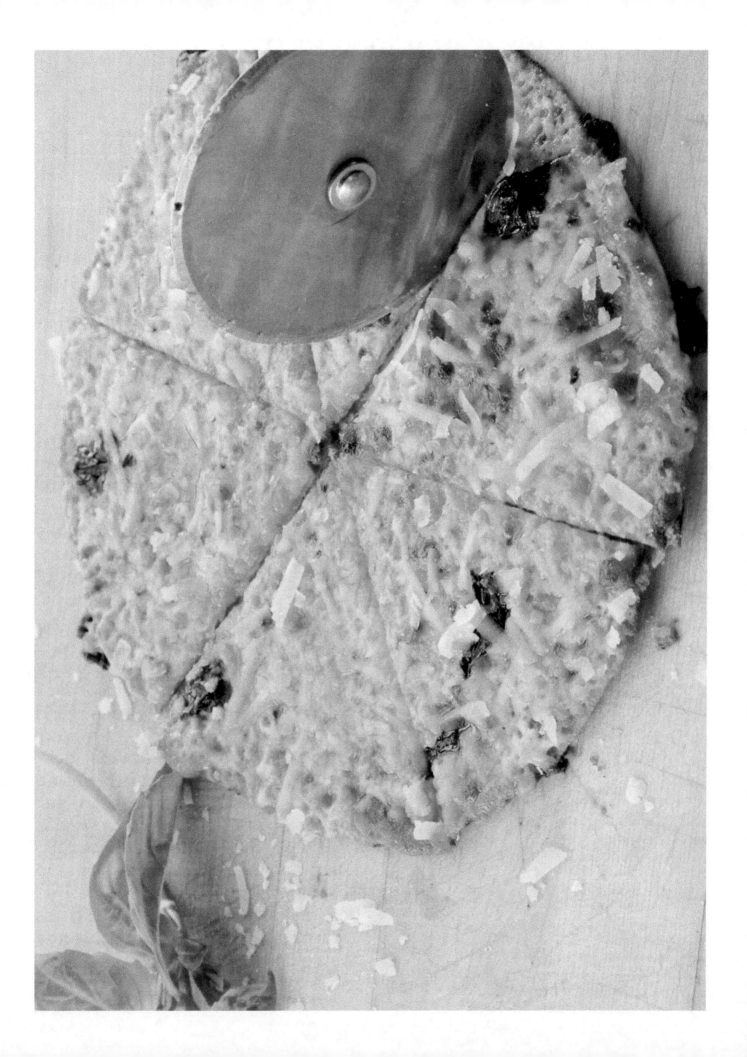

EXTRA-CRISPY BAR-STYLE TORTILLA PIZZA

YIELD: serves 1 to 2   **TOTAL TIME:** 15 minutes

ACTIVE TIME: 15 minutes

INGREDIENTS

- 1/2 teaspoon extra-virgin olive oil, plus more for drizzling
- 1 (10-inch) flour tortilla
- 1/4 cup store-bought or homemade pizza sauce
- 1 1/2 ounces shredded whole milk low moisture mozzarella cheese
- 1 ounce grated Parmesan cheese, divided
- 2 basil leaves, roughly torn
- Kosher salt

DIRECTIONS

1. Adjust oven rack to 6 to 8 inches below broiler element and preheat broiler to high. Heat oil in a large cast iron skillet over high heat until shimmering. Reduce heat to medium-low and wipe out excess oil with a paper towel.

2. Place tortilla in skillet with the rougher textured-side facing down. Spread sauce evenly over tortilla all the way to the edges. Spread mozzarella and half of Parmesan evenly over tortilla all the way to the edges. Season lightly with salt. Scatter with basil and drizzle with olive oil.

3. Place skillet under broiler and broil until cheese is melted and starting to brown in spots, 2 to 4 minutes. Remove from oven and sprinkle with remaining Parmesan. Using a small metal spatula, gently pry edges of pizza, releasing the cheese from the skillet. Peek under bottom. If more crispness is desired, place skillet over medium heat and cook, swirling pizza and peeking occasionally, until desired crispness is achieved. Slide pizza out onto a cutting board. Cut and serve immediately.

SOUTHERN-STYLE UNSWEETENED CORNBREAD RECIPE

YIELD: serves 1   **TOTAL TIME:** 1 hours

ACTIVE TIME: 20 minutes

INGREDIENTS

- 15 ounces (3 cups) stone-ground cornmeal (see note)
- 2 teaspoons kosher salt
- 2 teaspoons baking powder
- 3/4 teaspoon baking soda
- 3 teaspoons sugar (optional; see note)
- 2 1/2 cups buttermilk
- 3 eggs
- 1 1/2 sticks unsalted butter, melted, divided

DIRECTIONS

1. Place a well-seasoned 12-inch cast iron skillet on the center rack of the oven and preheat oven to 375°F.

2. Meanwhile, in a large bowl, whisk cornmeal with salt, baking powder, baking soda, and sugar (if using).

3. In a separate bowl, whisk buttermilk with eggs until homogenous. Whisking constantly, drizzle in all but 1 tablespoon melted butter.

4. Whisk liquid ingredients into dry ingredients just until thoroughly mixed; avoid over-mixing.

5. Pour remaining 1 tablespoon melted butter into preheated skillet and carefully swirl to coat bottom and sides. Scrape batter into prepared skillet, smoothing the top gently with a rubber spatula. Bake until cornbread is lightly browned on top and a skewer inserted into center comes out clean, about 45 minutes.

6. Let cool for about 15 minutes in skillet, then serve warm. (Cornbread does not keep well and will lose its texture as it cools, so it's best to eat it while it's still fresh.)

MOIST AND TENDER BROWN BUTTER CORNBREAD RECIPE

YIELD: serves 4 to 6   **TOTAL TIME:** 0 hours 30 minutes

ACTIVE TIME: 30 minutes

INGREDIENTS

- 7 tablespoons unsalted butter, plus more for serving
- 1 cup (about 5 ounces) fine yellow cornmeal
- 1 cup (about 5 ounces) all-purpose flour
- 4 tablespoons sugar
- 1 teaspoon kosher salt
- 2 teaspoons baking powder
- 1/4 teaspoon baking soda
- 2 eggs
- 6 ounces (about 3/4 cup) sour cream
- 4 ounces (about 1/2 cup) cultured buttermilk
- Honey, for serving

DIRECTIONS

1. Adjust oven rack to center position and preheat oven to 425°F. Place butter in a 10-inch cast iron skillet. Transfer skillet to oven and heat until the butter is melted and well browned, 10 to 20 minutes (you can measure your wet and dry ingredients while waiting). Pour browned butter into a heatproof cup or bowl, leaving about 1 tablespoon remaining in skillet.

2. Combine cornmeal, flour, sugar, salt, baking powder, and baking soda in a large bowl. Combine eggs, sour cream, and buttermilk in a second bowl and whisk until homogenous. Whisking constantly, slowly drizzle in reserved browned butter. Whisk wet ingredients into dry ingredients until homogenous.

3. Remove skillet from the oven and swirl to coat all surfaces with melted butter. Spoon batter into skillet, smooth top lightly, then transfer to oven. Bake until light golden brown on top and a wooden skewer inserted into cornbread comes out with no crumbs, 20 to 25 minutes. Let cool 10 minutes, then serve with extra butter and honey at the table. Leftover cornbread can be stored in a sealed container in the refrigerator for up to 3 days.

6. Let cool 15 minutes, then serve with sour cream.

1 cup (about 5 ounces) fine yellow cornmeal

1 cup (about 5 ounces) all-purpose flour

4 tablespoons sugar

2 teaspoons baking powder

1/4 teaspoon baking soda

2 eggs

6 ounces (about 3/4 cup) sour cream

4 ounces (about 1/4 cup) cultured buttermilk

Sour cream, for serving

4. For the Brown Butter Cornbread Crust: Combine cornmeal, flour, sugar, 1 teaspoon kosher salt, baking powder, and baking soda in a large bowl. Combine eggs, sour cream, and buttermilk in a second bowl and whisk until homogenous. Whisking constantly, slowly drizzle in reserved browned butter.

5. Using a large spoon, place small dollops of the cornbread batter mixture on top of the beef filling, then use the back of the spoon to spread it into an even layer. Transfer the skillet to the oven and bake until pale golden brown and a skewer inserted into the cornbread comes out clean, about 20 minutes.

QUICK AND EASY SKILLET TAMALE PIE WITH BROWN BUTTER CORNBREAD CRUST RECIPE

YIELD: serves 4 to 6   **TOTAL TIME:** 0 hours 45 minutes

ACTIVE TIME: 25 minutes

INGREDIENTS

- 6 tablespoons unsalted butter
- 1 pound ground beef chuck
- 1 medium onion, diced (about 1 cup)
- 4 medium cloves garlic, thinly sliced
- 2 tablespoons ancho chili powder
- 1/4 teaspoons cayenne pepper (optional)
- 1 tablespoon ground cumin
- 1 teaspoon ground coriander
- 1 cup frozen or fresh corn kernels, thawed if frozen
- 1 (15-ounce) can black beans, drained and rinsed
- 1 (28-ounce) can whole peeled tomatoes, drained and crushed with your hand through fingers to roughly break up
- 1 cup homemade chicken stock or low-sodium broth
- 4 ounces grated sharp cheddar cheese (about 1 cup)
- 3 scallions, thinly sliced
- 1/2 cup fresh cilantro leaves and fine stems, minced
- Kosher salt and freshly ground black pepper

For the Brown Butter Cornbread Crust:

DIRECTIONS

1. Adjust oven rack to center position and preheat oven to 425°F. Heat butter in a 12-inch cast iron or stainless steel skillet over medium heat until melted. Continue to cook, swirling pan gently until butter is nutty-smelling and solids are a toasty brown. Transfer to a heat-proof cup or bowl and reserve for Brown Butter Cornbread Crust.

2. Return pan to high heat. Add beef and cook, stirring and breaking up with a wooden spoon or a potato masher until starting to brown, about 8 minutes. Add onion and garlic and cook, stirring frequently, until softened and fragrant, about 4 minutes. Add chili powder, cayenne (if using), cumin, and coriander. Stir until fragrant, about 30 seconds.

3. Add corn, black beans, tomatoes, and chicken stock. Bring to a simmer, then stir in cheese. Reduce heat to low and cook, stirring occasionally, until thickened into a rich stew-like consistency, about 5 minutes. Remove from heat and stir in scallions and cilantro. Season to taste with salt and pepper.

4. Arrange salmon on top of leeks, skin side up, and transfer to oven. Cook salmon until an instant-read thermometer registers 110°F (43°C) in the very center for rare, 120°F (49°C) for medium-rare, or 130°F (54°C) for medium, 5 to 7 minutes.

5. Meanwhile, in a medium bowl, whisk together yogurt, cucumber, garlic, and herbs. Season with salt and pepper, then add lemon juice, 1 teaspoon at a time, to taste. (Yogurt sauce can also be made in advance and refrigerated up to 5 hours before serving.)

6. Transfer salmon and curried leeks to plates and spoon cold yogurt sauce alongside. Serve.

ONE-SKILLET SALMON WITH CURRIED LEEKS AND YOGURT-HERB SAUCE RECIPE

YIELD: serves 4
TOTAL TIME: 0 hours 35 minutes
ACTIVE TIME: 35 minutes

INGREDIENTS

- 4 (6-ounce; 170g) skin-on, center-cut salmon fillets
- Kosher salt and freshly ground black pepper
- 4 tablespoons (60ml) extra-virgin olive oil, divided
- 3 pounds leeks (1.4kg; about 4 medium leeks), white and light green parts only, cut into long, thin strips (about 4 inches by 1/4 inch)
- 1 1/2 teaspoons curry powder
- 3/4 cup (180ml) yogurt
- 1 (4-ounce; 115g) piece English cucumber (from one 10-ounce cucumber), peeled and very finely minced or grated
- 1 small clove garlic, minced
- 1 packed tablespoon minced fresh herbs, such as mint, dill, and/or parsley
- Juice of 1 lemon, to taste

DIRECTIONS

1. Preheat oven to 325°F (163°C). Dry salmon very well with paper towels, then season all over with salt and pepper. In a large cast iron, carbon steel, or stainless steel skillet, heat 2 tablespoons (30ml) oil over medium-high heat until shimmering. Reduce heat to medium-low, then add a salmon fillet, skin side down. Press firmly in place for 10 seconds, using the back of a flexible fish spatula, to prevent skin from buckling. Add remaining fillets one at a time, pressing each with spatula for 10 seconds, until all fillets are in the pan.

2. Cook, pressing gently on back of fillets occasionally to ensure skin makes good contact with pan, until skin releases easily from pan and is crispy, about 6 minutes. Transfer salmon, skin side up, to a platter and set aside.

3. Add remaining 2 tablespoons (30ml) oil to skillet and heat over medium-high heat until shimmering. Add leeks and cook, stirring, until they begin to soften and compress (tongs can help move them around more efficiently), about 3 minutes. Add curry powder and stir well to combine. Continue cooking until leeks are very tender, about 6 to 8 minutes longer. Lower heat at any point to prevent scorching. Season with salt and pepper (be careful, as some curry powders contain salt).

5. Add honey to sauce, stirring to combine; taste, then add more honey as desired to balance the tartness of the plums (this will depend on the plums you have). Stir in butter until melted. Remove from heat. Discard thyme sprigs.

6. Spoon sauce onto serving plates, arrange quail on top, and serve. You can garnish with minced parsley, if desired.

PAN-ROASTED QUAIL WITH PLUM PAN SAUCE RECIPE

YIELD: serves 4
TOTAL TIME: 0 hours 35 minutes
ACTIVE TIME: 35 minutes

INGREDIENTS

- 4 whole quail, deboned or spatchcocked
- Kosher salt
- 2 tablespoons (30ml) vegetable oil
- One medium shallot, minced (1 1/2-ounces, 40g; about 1/4 cup minced)
- 2 sprigs fresh thyme
- 4 small Italian plums (about 8 ounces), pitted and diced
- 1 cup (235ml) water or quail stock or homemade chicken stock or store-bought low-sodium chicken broth (see note)
- 1 tablespoon (15ml) honey, plus more as needed
- 2 tablespoons (30g) unsalted butter
- Minced flat-leaf parsley, for garnish (optional)

DIRECTIONS

1. Season quail all over with salt. In a large cast iron skillet, heat oil over medium-high heat until shimmering. Add quail. If quail are spatchcocked, cook them skin side down until well browned, about 5 minutes, then flip and cook other side until desired doneness is reached (quail can be served from medium-rare to well done, as desired; they are too small to accurately use a thermometer, so feel free to cut into the meat to check doneness). If using deboned quail, cook on both sides, turning frequently, until browned on both sides and desired doneness is reach, about 4 minutes per side for medium.

2. Transfer quail to a plate or wire rack set over a rimmed baking sheet to rest.

3. Add shallot and thyme to skillet and cook, stirring, until shallot is softened, about 3 minutes. Add plums and cook, stirring, until starting to look pulpy, about 4 minutes.

4. Add water or stock to pan, bring to a simmer, then cook until liquid has reduced and plums have broken down to form a thick sauce. Add any juices that have collected below quail. Season with salt.

PAN-SEARED FLANK STEAK WITH PEACHES AND DANDELION GREENS RECIPE

YIELD: serves 2   **TOTAL TIME:** 0 hours 15 minutes

ACTIVE TIME: 15 minutes

INGREDIENTS

- One 1- to 1 1/2-pound (450 to 680g) flank steak
- Kosher salt and freshly ground black pepper, to taste
- 2 tablespoons vegetable oil or other neutral oil (1 ounce; 30g)
- 2 to 3 sprigs fresh thyme
- 3 garlic cloves
- 2 tablespoons butter (1 ounce; 30g)
- 1 large peach (about 7 ounces; 200g), cut into 8 wedges
- 1 tablespoon chopped Calabrian chili (1/2 ounce; 15g)
- 2 tablespoons lemon juice (1 ounce; 30g), from 1/2 lemon
- 1 bunch dandelion greens (about 6 ounces; 170g)

DIRECTIONS

1. Preheat a 12-inch heavy-gauge skillet or cast iron pan over high heat. Season flank steak generously with kosher salt and freshly ground pepper. Heat oil in pan until smoking-hot before carefully placing steak in hot pan, laying it down away from you. Cook steak, pressing the thicker part down with an offset spatula, small pan, or cooking weight and flipping every 30 seconds, until it develops a deeply browned crust and internal temperature is about 15°F away from your desired final temperature, about 8 minutes. (We suggest cooking flank steak to medium doneness, or about 140°F/60°C.) Add thyme, garlic, and butter to pan and lower heat to medium. Using a large spoon, baste steak with butter until it is 5°F away from your desired final temperature, about 4 minutes. Remove steak to a sheet tray fitted with a wire rack, pouring butter and aromatics over steak. Set aside to rest.

2. Return same pan to high heat and place peaches in pan, pressing cut sides of peaches onto the brown bits developed from cooking the steak. Sear peaches until golden brown, about 1 minute.

3. Add 1/2 cup (120ml) water to pan and use it to scrape up all the browned bits from the pan to form a pan sauce. Add Calabrian chili, lemon juice, and 2 tablespoons of the steak drippings to the pan, simmering and swirling to emulsify the sauce. Add dandelion greens and cook until gently wilted, about 1 minute. Slice steak and serve right away with greens, peaches, and sauce.

1 teaspoon freshly ground black pepper

1 1/2 cups (8 ounces) grated Gruyère cheese

4. lButter a 12-inch cast iron skillet or a 9- by 13-inch baking dish and add half of bread. Scatter half of caramelized onions and half of cheese all over. Layer remaining bread on top and scatter remaining onions and cheese over. Drizzle any remaining custard all over, then bake until bread is crisp and custard is just set, about 35 minutes. Serve hot or at room temperature.

FRENCH ONION STRATA (SAVORY BREAD PUDDING) RECIPE

YIELD: 6

TOTAL TIME: 1 hours 15 minutes

ACTIVE TIME: 40 minutes

INGREDIENTS

For the Caramelized Onions:

3 tablespoons (45g) unsalted butter, plus more for greasing baking dish

3 large Spanish onions (about 2 1/2 pounds; 1kg), thinly sliced

1 teaspoon sugar

1 teaspoon kosher salt

3 medium cloves garlic, minced

2 teaspoons finely chopped fresh thyme leaves

1/4 cup (60ml) dry sherry

1/2 cup (120ml) dry white wine

For the Strata:

1 large Italian or French bread loaf (about 1 pound; 450g), cut into 1-inch cubes

6 large eggs

3 1/2 cups (830ml) half and half or whole milk

1 1/2 tablespoons (22ml) smooth Dijon mustard

1 tablespoon (15ml) Worcestershire sauce

1 teaspoon (5ml) fish sauce (optional)

1/2 teaspoon kosher salt

DIRECTIONS

1. For the Caramelized Onions: In a large skillet, melt butter over medium heat, then add onions, sugar, and 1 teaspoon salt. Cover and cook, stirring every few minutes, until onions have softened, about 10 minutes. Remove lid and cook, stirring frequently and keeping skillet uncovered, until onions are deep golden brown, 20 to 25 minutes; if onions threaten to burn at any point, stir in a tablespoon or two of water as needed, and/or lower heat. Add garlic and thyme and cook 1 minute longer. Add sherry and wine and cook until liquid has almost completely evaporated, about 3 minutes. Remove from heat and set aside.

2. Meanwhile, for the Strata: Preheat oven to 350°F (177°C). Spread bread in a single layer on a baking sheet. Bake until bread is dry but not browned, about 8 minutes.

3. In a large bowl, whisk together eggs, half and half or milk, mustard, Worcestershire sauce, fish sauce (if using), 1/2 teaspoon salt, and pepper. Add dried bread and let soak in custard for at least 15 minutes and up to 30 minutes.

2 teaspoons (10ml) Dijon mustard

3/4 cup grated Gruyère cheese (2 1/2 ounces; 75g)

4 to 6 large eggs

Pinch of red chili flakes, for garnish

4 to 6 slices toasted and buttered bread, such as from a baguette

5. Using a spoon, make egg-sized indentations in greens, one for each egg. Crack an egg into each well and season with salt. Bake until egg whites are just set and yolks are still runny, 10 to 20 minutes. Check eggs frequently to make sure they don't overcook.

3. Add remaining 2 tablespoons (30g) butter to skillet and melt over medium-high heat until foaming. Add leeks and cook, stirring often, until softened but not browned. Stir in minced garlic and cook 30 seconds. Sprinkle flour over leeks and cook, stirring, until raw flour smell has cooked off, about 1 minute. Stir in half and half and milk. Bring to a simmer and cook until sauce thickens, 1 to 2 minutes. Stir in wine, nutmeg, mustard, reserved mushrooms, and reserved greens and return to a simmer. Season with salt and pepper. Remove skillet from heat. If mixture is very thick, add a bit more water or milk to thin slightly.

BAKED EGGS WITH CREAMY GREENS, MUSHROOMS, AND CHEESE RECIPE

YIELD: serves 4 to 6   **TOTAL TIME:** 0 hours 50 minutes

ACTIVE TIME: 30 minutes

INGREDIENTS

Kosher salt

1 large bunch lacinato kale, tough stems removed, leaves roughly chopped (about 6 ounces; 180g after stemming)

1 large bunch Swiss chard, tough stems removed, leaves roughly chopped (about 7 ounces; 200g after stemming)

5 ounces (140g) baby spinach

3 tablespoons (45g) unsalted butter, divided

8 ounces (225g) button or cremini mushrooms, stems trimmed and caps sliced

Freshly ground black pepper

2 leeks, white and light green parts only, washed well and thinly sliced (about 9 ounces; 250g total)

3 medium cloves garlic, 2 minced or grated and 1 left whole for toast, divided

2 tablespoons (45g) all-purpose flour

1 cup (235ml) half and half

1/2 cup (120ml) milk

3 tablespoons (45ml) dry white wine

1/8 teaspoon freshly grated nutmeg

DIRECTIONS

1. Preheat oven to 375°F (190°C). Bring a large pot of salted water to a boil. Working in batches if necessary, add kale, chard, and spinach to pot and cook for 1 minute. Using a spider or strainer, lift greens from water and transfer to a colander. Immediately run under cold water to stop the cooking. Repeat with remaining greens if necessary. Using your hands, squeeze greens to remove as much excess liquid as possible. Roughly chop greens and set aside. You should have about 10 1/2 ounces (300g) of cooked, squeezed greens.

2. In a large skillet, melt 1 tablespoon (15g) butter over medium-high heat until foaming. Add mushrooms and cook, stirring only occasionally, until well browned, about 6 minutes. Season with salt and pepper, then transfer to a plate.

4. If baking in the same skillet, sprinkle Gruyère on top of greens. If using a baking dish, scrape creamy greens into it, smooth into an even layer, and sprinkle Gruyère on top.

6. While toast is still warm, gently rub one side of each slice with remaining clove of garlic. Serve, using toast to scoop up greens and eggs. about 4 cups of creamed greens.

4. Scrape yogurt mixture from the skillet into a heatproof measuring cup. If needed, stir in enough water to bring the total volume up to 1 cup. Return 1 cup of the yogurt mixture to the skillet and broil until boiling, about 2 minutes.

5. Add the couscous to the skillet, scatter dates on top and cover skillet to allow couscous to steam in the hot liquid for 5 minutes. Uncover. Either directly in the skillet or in a serving bowl, toss couscous with half the toasted almonds, half the parsley, and the remaining lemon juice. Top with the chicken, garnish with the remaining almonds and parsley, and serve.

BROILED TANDOORI-STYLE CHICKEN WITH ALMONDS AND COUSCOUS RECIPE

YIELD: serves 2 - 4　　**TOTAL TIME:** 0 hours 30 minutes

ACTIVE TIME: 30 minutes

INGREDIENTS

- 8 ounces (225g) yogurt
- 2 ounces (60ml) fresh lemon juice, divided
- 1 tablespoon tandoori spice blend, such as Penzey's
- Kosher salt
- 1 pound (450g) boneless, skinless chicken thighs, cut into 1/2-inch pieces
- 1/2 cup (2 1/2 ounces; 70g) slivered almonds
- 1 cup (5 1/2 ounces; 150g) dry couscous
- 1/3 cup (1 3/4 ounces; 50g) pitted dates, chopped
- 1/2 cup roughly chipped flat-leaf parsley, for garnish
- 6 large eggs
- 3 1/2 cups (830ml) half and half or whole milk
- 1 1/2 tablespoons (22ml) smooth Dijon mustard

DIRECTIONS

1. In a mixing bowl, stir together yogurt, 1 ounce (30ml) lemon juice, and tandoori spices. Season with salt. In a plastic zipper-top bag, combine chicken and yogurt mixture and mix thoroughly to coat. Marinate in the refrigerator for at least 1 hour and up to 8 hours.

2. Turn on broiler and set oven rack about 6 inches from broiler element. In a large cast iron or stainless steel skillet, toast the almonds under the broiler until slightly browned, about 2 minutes (check frequently as broilers can vary considerably). Remove almonds from the pan and set them aside.

3. Scrape chicken and yogurt marinade into the same skillet. Broil, turning once, until chicken is browned on both sides and just cooked through, about 6 minutes per side (again, check frequently as broilers vary). Using a slotted spoon, remove chicken pieces from the skillet and set aside in a warm place.

Warmed corn or flour tortillas

Lime wedges

Homemade or store-bought salsa verde (optional)

3. Wipe out skillet, return it to stovetop, and lower heat to medium. Add 1 tablespoon plus 2 teaspoons (25ml) pork fat and pulled roast pork shoulder to now-empty skillet, and arrange pork in a single layer. Season lightly with salt and pepper, and cook, stirring occasionally, until pork is golden brown and crisp on all sides, 8 to 10 minutes. Using a slotted spoon, transfer pork to a plate and set aside.

4. Add remaining 2 tablespoons (30ml) pork fat (or vegetable oil) to skillet and increase heat to medium-high. Add potatoes and arrange in as even a single layer as possible. Season lightly with salt, and cook, stirring and tossing occasionally, until potatoes are deep brown and crisp on all sides, about 20 minutes. Add coriander, chili powder, and cumin and cook, stirring frequently, until fragrant, about 30 seconds. Return pork, asparagus, and serrano to the skillet, along with any drippings reserved from roast pork shoulder (if you have saved them), toss to combine, and continue to cook until all components are heated through, about 2 minutes. Season with salt and pepper.

5. For Serving: Sprinkle scallions and/or cilantro over the hash, and top with fried eggs. Serve right away, passing warmed tortillas, lime, and salsa verde at the table.

CRISPY PORK SHOULDER HASH WITH CHARRED ASPARAGUS AND SERRANO CHILI RECIPE

YIELD: serves 4
TOTAL TIME: 0 hours 50 minutes
ACTIVE TIME: 30 minutes

INGREDIENTS

For the Hash:

1 1/2 pounds (675g) Yukon gold or russet potatoes, cut into 3/4-inch dice (see note)

2 tablespoons (30ml) distilled white vinegar

Kosher salt and freshly ground black pepper

10 ounces (285g) asparagus (about 1 bunch), woody ends trimmed

1 fresh serrano chili (about 10g)

1/4 cup (60ml) rendered pork fat from roast pork shoulder or vegetable oil, divided (see note)

12 ounces (340g) roast pork shoulder, pulled into 2-inch long pieces (see note)

1/2 teaspoon ground coriander

1/4 teaspoon chili powder

1/4 teaspoon ground cumin

Reserved drippings from roast pork shoulder (optional)

For Serving:

Thinly sliced scallions and/or roughly chopped fresh cilantro leaves and tender stems

Fried eggs (optional)

DIRECTIONS

1. For the Hash: Place potatoes in a 3-quart saucepan and cover with 2 quarts cold water. Add vinegar and 2 tablespoons kosher salt. Bring to a boil over high heat. Reduce to a simmer and cook until barely tender, about 7 minutes after coming to a boil. Drain potatoes in a colander, then set aside.

2. Meanwhile, heat a large cast iron skillet over high heat for 5 minutes. Add asparagus and serrano to the pan and arrange in a single layer. Cook, turning occasionally until asparagus and serrano are charred all over and asparagus is just cooked through, 4 to 6 minutes for thin spears, 5 to 8 minutes for thick spears. Carefully add 1 teaspoon (5ml) pork fat (or vegetable oil) to the skillet, toss to coat vegetables, and season lightly with salt and pepper. Transfer vegetables to cutting board. Once vegetables are cool enough to handle, cut asparagus into 2-inch pieces and de-seed and finely mince the serrano. Set aside.

3 ounces grated Parmigiano-Reggiano (1 cup; 85g)

1/4 cup (10g) chopped fresh flat-leaf parsley leaves

5. Meanwhile, in a pot of salted boiling water, cook pasta. If using dry pasta, cook until just shy of al dente (1 to 2 minutes less than the package directs). If using fresh pasta, cook until noodles are barely cooked through. Using either a spider skimmer (for short pasta) or tongs (for long fresh pasta), transfer pasta to pan with mushrooms along with 3/4 cup (180ml) pasta cooking water. Alternatively, drain pasta using a colander or fine-mesh strainer, making sure to reserve at least 2 cups (475ml) pasta cooking water.

6. Heat sauce and pasta over high and cook, stirring and tossing rapidly, until pasta is al dente (fresh pasta will never be truly al dente) and sauce is thickened and coats noodles, 1 to 2 minutes, adding more pasta cooking water in 1/4 cup (60ml) increments as needed. At this point, the sauce should coat the pasta but still be loose enough to pool around the edges of the pan. Add the butter, and stir and toss rapidly to melt and emulsify into the sauce. Remove from heat, add 3/4 of grated cheese and all of the parsley, and stir rapidly to incorporate. Season with salt to taste. Serve immediately, passing remaining grated cheese at the table.

CREAMY PASTA WITH MUSHROOMS (PASTA AI FUNGHI) RECIPE

YIELD: serves 4

TOTAL TIME: 0 hours 30 minutes

ACTIVE TIME: 30 minutes

INGREDIENTS

- 1 cup (240ml) homemade or store-bought low sodium chicken stock (see note)
- 1 1/2 teaspoons (4g) powdered gelatin, such as Knox
- 2 tablespoons (30ml) extra-virgin olive oil
- 1 1/2 pounds (675g) mixed mushrooms (such as shiitake, oyster, maitake, beech, cremini, and chanterelles), cleaned, trimmed, and thinly sliced or torn by hand (see note)
- Kosher salt and freshly ground black pepper
- 3 medium shallots, finely minced (about 3/4 cup; 120g)
- 2 medium (10g) garlic cloves, minced
- 2 tablespoons (4g) chopped fresh thyme leaves
- 1/2 cup (120ml) dry white wine or 1/4 cup (60ml) dry sherry
- 1 teaspoon (5ml) fish sauce (optional)
- 1 pound (450g) short dried pasta (such as casarecce or gemelli) or long fresh egg-dough pasta (such as tagliatelle or fettuccine)
- 6 tablespoons unsalted butter (3 ounces; 85g)

DIRECTIONS

1. Pour stock into small small bowl or liquid measuring cup and evenly sprinkle gelatin over surface of stock. Set aside.

2. In a large 12-inch cast iron or stainless steel skillet, heat oil over medium-high heat until shimmering. Add mushrooms, season with salt and pepper, and cook, stirring frequently with a wooden spoon, until moisture has evaporated and mushrooms are deeply browned, 12 to 15 minutes.

3. Add shallots, garlic, and thyme and cook, stirring constantly, until fragrant and shallots are softened, 30 seconds to 1 minute. Add wine or sherry, and cook, swirling pan and scraping up any stuck-on bits with a wooden spoon, until wine is reduced by half, about 30 seconds.

4. Add chicken stock mixture, season lightly with salt, and bring to a simmer. Reduce heat to medium-low, add fish sauce (if using), and cook, stirring occasionally, until mushroom mixture is thickened to a saucy consistency, about 5 minutes. Turn off heat.

CRISPY CHEESE- AND KIMCHI-TOPPED SKILLET RICE RECIPE

YIELD: serves 4   **TOTAL TIME:** 0 hours 50 minutes

ACTIVE TIME: 10 minutes

INGREDIENTS

- 1 tablespoon (15g) unsalted butter, softened
- 4 cups cooked short-grain rice (see note)
- 3 tablespoons (45ml) gochujang
- 3 tablespoons (45ml) soy sauce
- 1 tablespoon (15ml) rice vinegar
- 4 thinly sliced scallions (~80g), white and green parts divided
- 3 ounces (85g) grated low-moisture mozzarella cheese (see note), divided
- 5 ounces (141g) chopped drained kimchi (see note)
- 1 ounce (28g) grated Cotija cheese (see note)

5. Place pan under broiler for about 2 minutes, or until Gruyère and mozzarella melt and bubble and Cotija begins to char in spots. Remove pan from under broiler, top with sliced scallion greens, and serve immediately.

DIRECTIONS

1. Preheat oven to 400°F (200°C). Grease a 10-inch cast iron pan with 1 tablespoon (15g) butter, making sure to fully cover both the bottom

2. In a medium mixing bowl, combine rice, gochujang, soy sauce, rice vinegar, and sliced scallion whites. Using a flexible spatula, mix thoroughly.

3. Scrape half of rice mixture into buttered cast iron skillet and, using the bottom of a drinking glass or measuring cup, press down firmly to create a single even layer of seasoned rice. Distribute half of the mozzarella and Gruyère over the layer of rice, then scrape the rest of the rice mixture over grated cheese. Using the bottom of a drinking glass or measuring cup, press down firmly to create an even top layer of seasoned rice. Transfer pan to oven and cook for 35 minutes.

4. Remove pan from oven. Turn off oven and turn broiler on high. While broiler preheats, top rice with chopped kimchi. Distribute remaining Gruyère and mozzarella over kimchi and sprinkle Cotija over the other cheeses.

PAN FRIED POTATOES

YIELDS: 3 to 4

COOK TIME: 0 hours 10 mins

PREP TIME: 0 hours 05 mins

DIET: vegan

INGREDIENTS

- 1 pound yellow or red potatoes
- 2 tablespoons olive oil
- 2 tablespoons butter (or 2 tablespoons olive oil, for vegan)
- 1/2 teaspoon kosher salt
- 1/2 teaspoon smoked paprika
- 1/4 teaspoon garlic powder
- 1/4 teaspoon dried thyme

DIRECTIONS

1. Wash the potatoes. Cut them into thin slices, about 1/4" inch thick.

2. Heat the butter and olive oil in a large skillet over medium high heat.

3. Add the potatoes and cook them for 10 to 12 minutes until browned, flipping occasionally until all sides are browned. Sprinkle with seasoning and serve hot.

BREAKFAST VEGETABLE SCRAMBLE

YIELDS: 2
PREP TIME: 0 hours 08 mins
COOK TIME: 0 hours 07 mins
DIET: vegetarian

INGREDIENTS

- 2 tablespoons olive oil
- 1/2 red onion
- 1 red bell pepper (or 1/2 red and 1/2 orange)
- 4 cups baby kale or spinach
- 1 tablespoon chopped chives or other fresh herbs
- 4 eggs or this Tofu Scramble
- 1/4 cup shredded Colby cheese or crumbled goat cheese (optional)
- 1/4 teaspoon kosher salt
- Fresh ground black pepper
- Avocado slices, for serving

DIRECTIONS

1. Prep the vegetables: Thinly slice the red onion. Large dice the bell pepper.

2. Prep the eggs or tofu: In a medium bowl, crack the eggs and whisk them together until well-beaten. Stir in the shredded cheese, fresh herbs, kosher salt, and plenty of fresh ground pepper. Or, complete Step 1 of the Tofu Scramble.

3. Cook the vegetables: Heat the olive oil in a large skillet over medium high heat. When hot, add the onion and peppers. Cook 3 to 4 minutes until tender and just starting to brown, stirring occasionally. Reduce heat to low. Add a pinch of salt and the baby greens. Cook for 30 seconds until wilted. Remove and set aside.

4. Cook the eggs or tofu: Keep heat on low. Pour in the eggs. Cook for 20 to 30 seconds. When the eggs just start to set, use a flat spatula to scrape sections of eggs, gently stirring constantly until cooked but still soft, about 1 minute. Or, complete Step 2 of the Tofu Scramble.

5. Add the vegetables and serve: Add the veggies back to the pan with the eggs or tofu. Stir for a few seconds until combined and warmed. Serve immediately.

EASY SHAKSHUKA WITH FETA

YIELDS: 4
PREP TIME: 0 hours 10 mins
COOK TIME: 0 hours 25 mins

INGREDIENTS

- 1 teaspoon coriander seeds*
- 1 teaspoon cumin seeds*
- 1 teaspoon fennel seeds*
- 2 tablespoons olive oil
- 1 red bell pepper
- 1 large yellow onion
- 1 teaspoon smoked paprika
- 1 teaspoon kosher salt, plus more for sprinkling
- 1 28 ounce can diced tomatoes
- 1 15 ounce can white beans, drained and rinsed
- 4 to 6 large eggs, to your preference
- Freshly ground black pepper
- 1/2 cup fresh parsley or cilantro leaves
- 1/2 cup feta cheese crumbles

DIRECTIONS

1. Thinly slice the pepper. Thinly slice the onion.

2. Set a dry skillet, preferably cast iron, over medium heat. Add the coriander, cumin, and fennel seeds, then toast until fragrant, about 2 minutes. Carefully transfer the seeds to a plate to cool, then grind in a mortar and pestle or spice grinder.

3. Heat the olive oil in the same skillet over medium-high heat. Add the bell pepper and onion in an even layer, then do not be tempted to stir or fuss with them. Let them get a good, dark char, 3 to 4 minutes, before giving a quick stir and cooking a bit more until nearly all of the pepper and onion are blackened in parts. This process will take about 10 minutes.

4. Add the ground spices, paprika, and kosher salt. Stir for 1 minute before carefully tipping in the tomatoes. Let this mixture come to a simmer before stirring in the white beans. Bring everything to a gently boil, then lower the heat to a steady simmer. Simmer for 5 minutes, or until the tomatoes have thickened.

5. Carve out a little divot for each of the eggs you plan to cook, then carefully crack them in. Add a bit of kosher salt and black pepper to each egg then cover the skillet with a lid (or sheet pan if you can't find a matching lid). Cook over low heat until the eggs are just set, 4 to 6 minutes.

6. Chop the cilantro. Finish by garnishing with the fresh herbs and feta. Serve immediately.

Printed in the USA
CPSIA information can be obtained
at www.ICGtesting.com
LVHW061947281124
797896LV00014B/1186